My God

Mel Calman

D1646457

Methuen

A Methuen Paperback

First published in Great Britain in 1970
by Souvenir Press Ltd
Re-issued in 1985
by Methuen London Ltd
11 New Fetter Lane, London EC4P 4EE
Copyright © 1970 and 1984 by Mel Calman
Cover and book designed by Philip Thompson

ISBN 0 413 57330 3

Some of these cartoons first appeared in the Sunday Times

Also by Mel Calman:

This Pestered Isle *(Times Newspapers Ltd)*
But it's my turn to leave you . . . *(Methuen)*
How about a little quarrel before bed? *(Methuen)*
Help! *(Methuen)*
Calman Revisited *(Methuen)*
The Big Novel *(Methuen)*
It's only you that's incompatible *(Methuen)*

To My God —
if He is still there . . .

Made and printed in Great Britain
by Richard Clay (The Chaucer Press) Ltd
Bungay, Suffolk

That's one of my favourite advertisements...

I could use a few
'Praise Hims' just now.

They love me,
they love me not—
they love me .

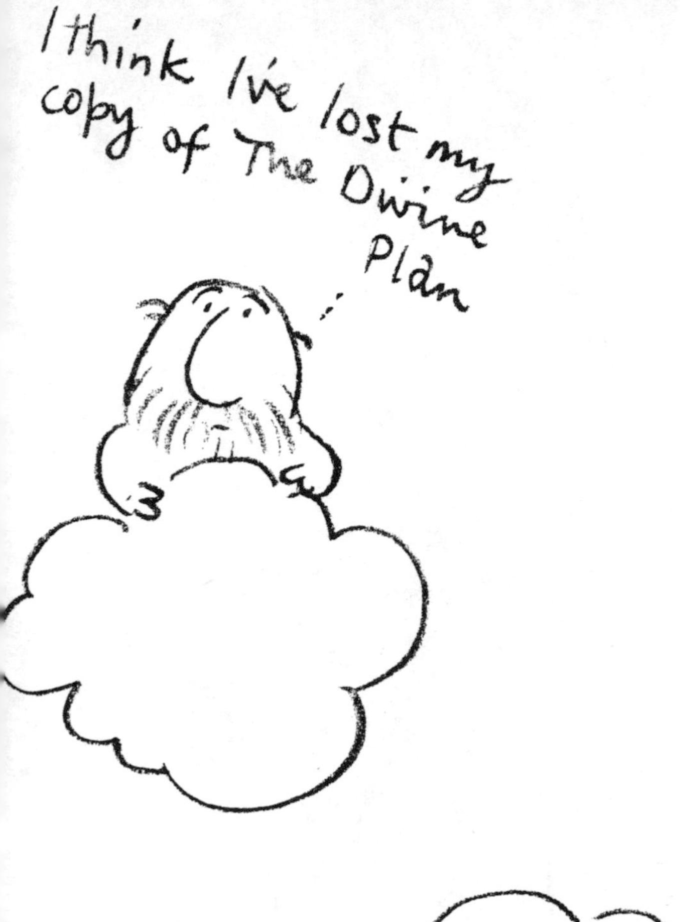
I think I've lost my copy of The Divine Plan

one week's work
and an eternity
of worry . .

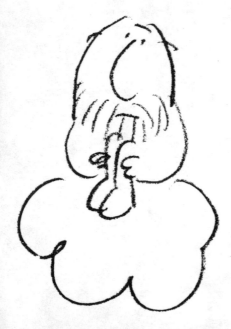

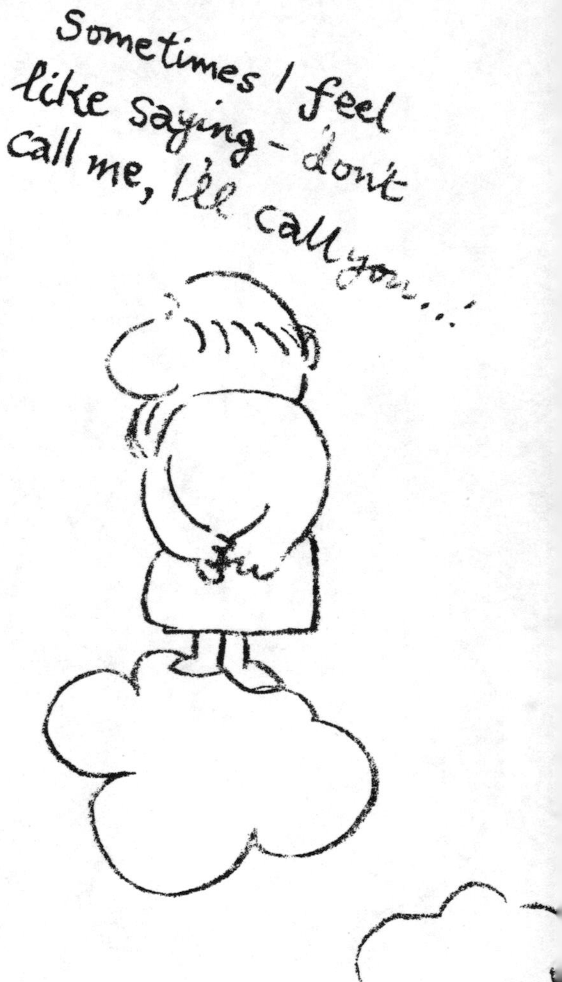
Sometimes I feel like saying – don't call me, I'll call you...!

Sometimes I wish
I hadn't gone into
the Deity...

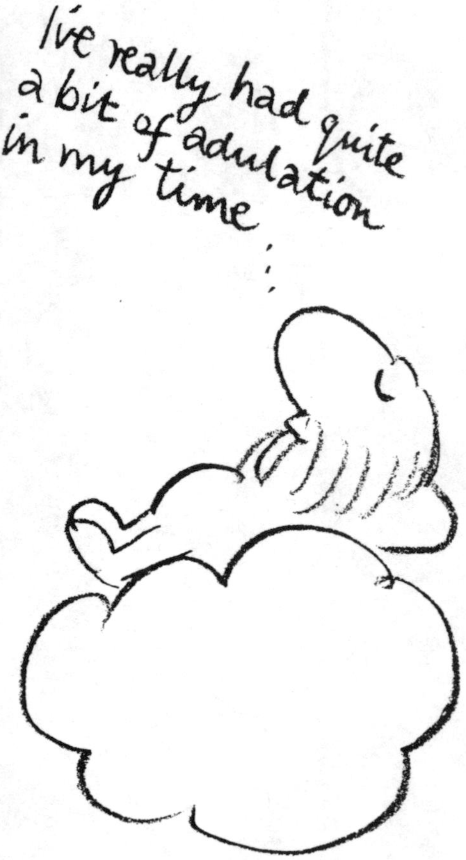
I've really had quite
a bit of adulation
in my time

In my position you have to be so careful what you say ...

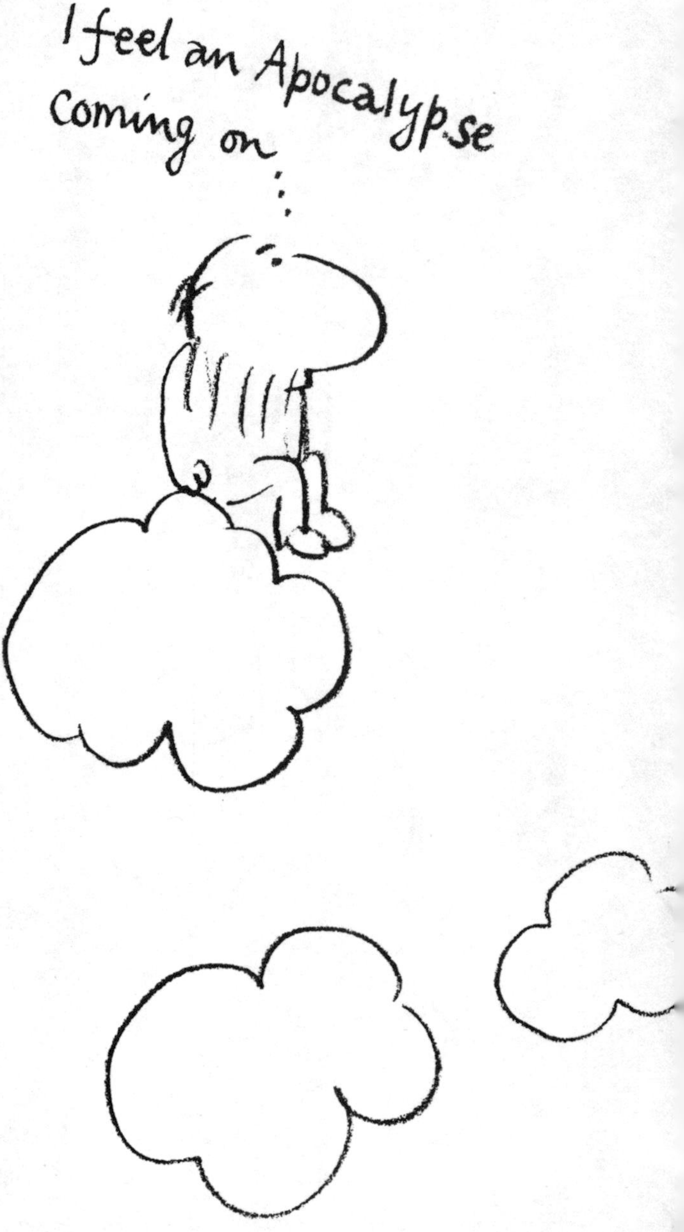
I feel an Apocalypse coming on . . .

Please God!

Help!

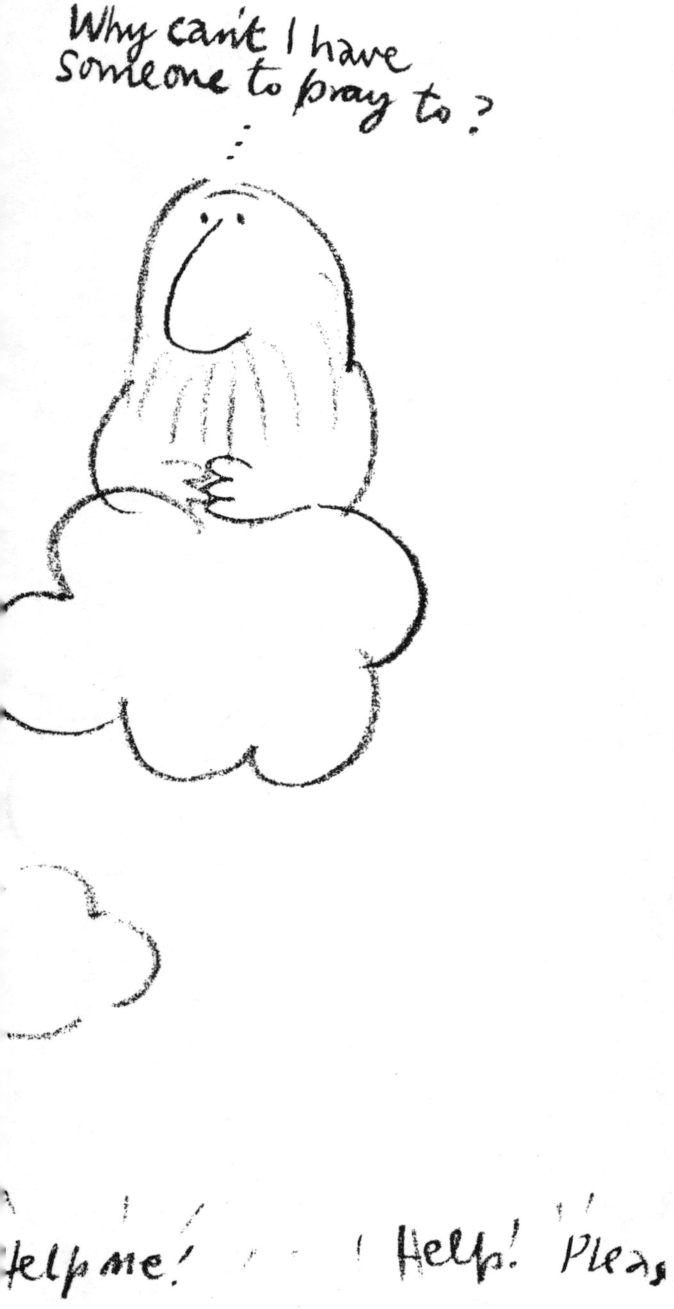
Why can't I have someone to pray to?
elp me!
Help! Pleas

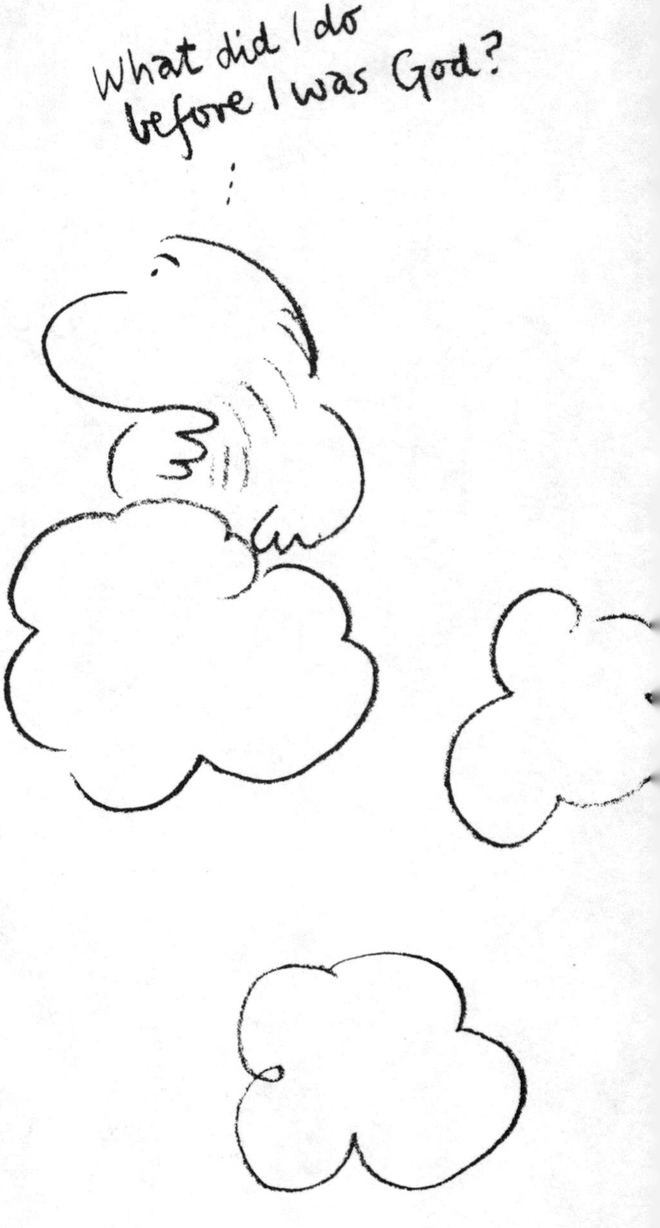
What did I do
before I was God?

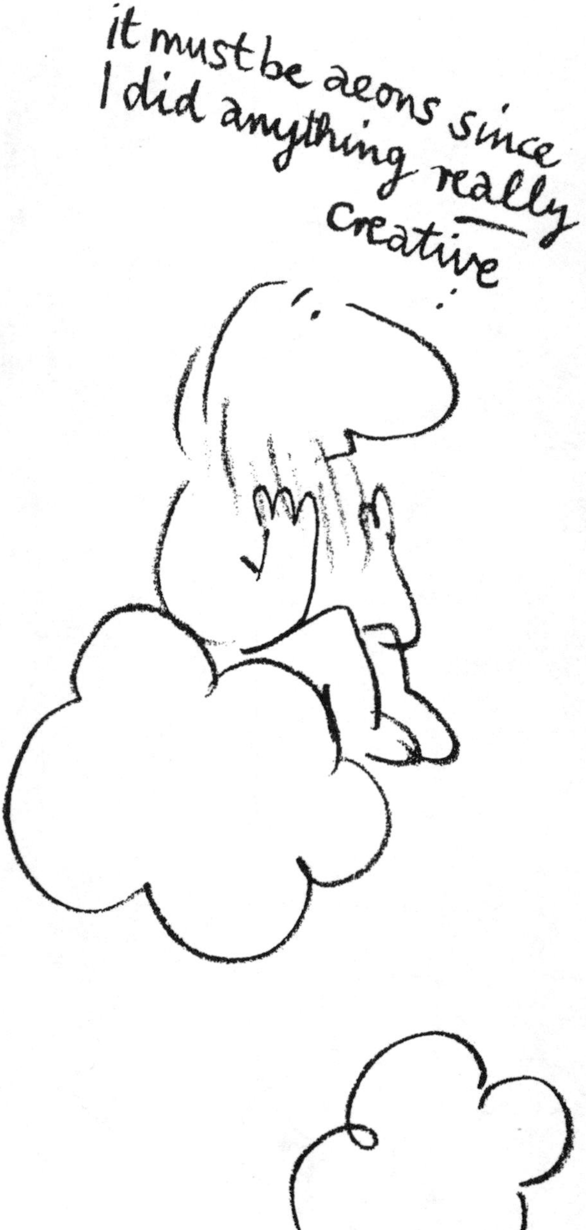
it must be aeons since
I did anything really
creative

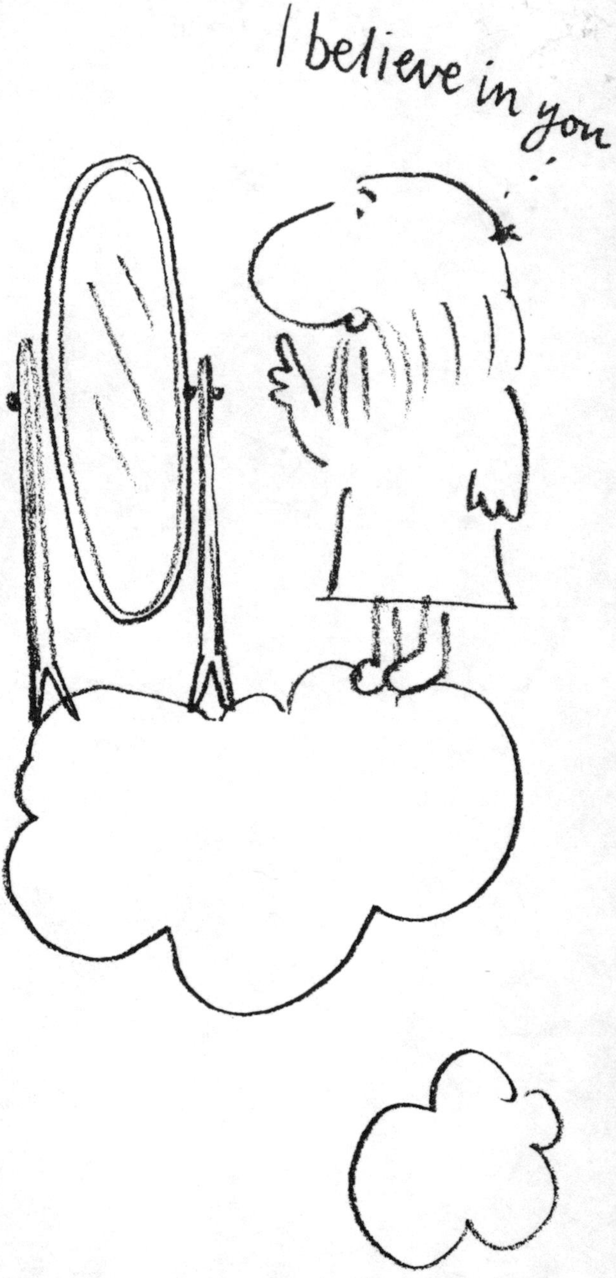
I believe in you

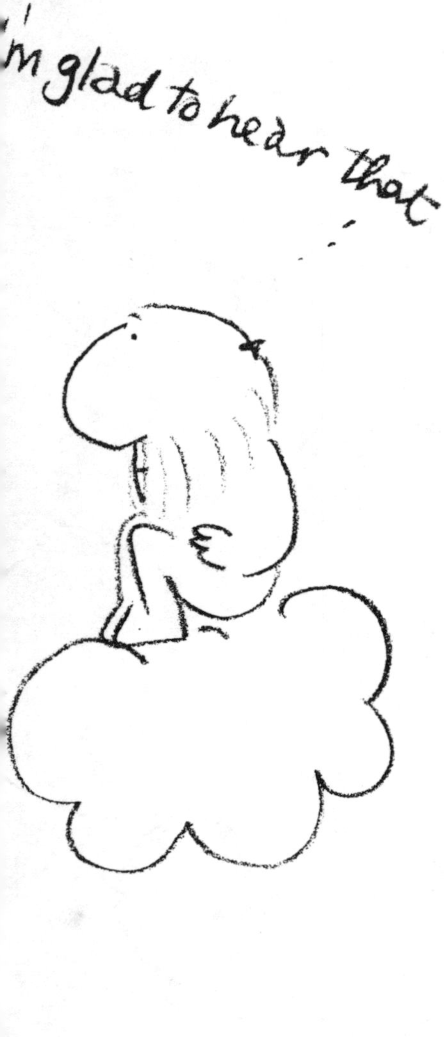
'm glad to hear that...

Being God isn't all nectar and thunderbolts, you know...

I may not be perfect but I'm better than nothing...

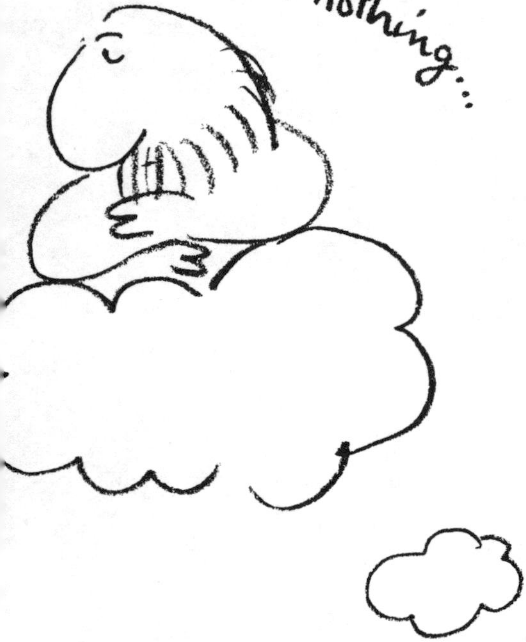

Of course, once you've
created The Universe
everything else you
seems an anti-cli

I really don't kno
what people se
in you...

Love one another
or I'll come down there
and thump you...

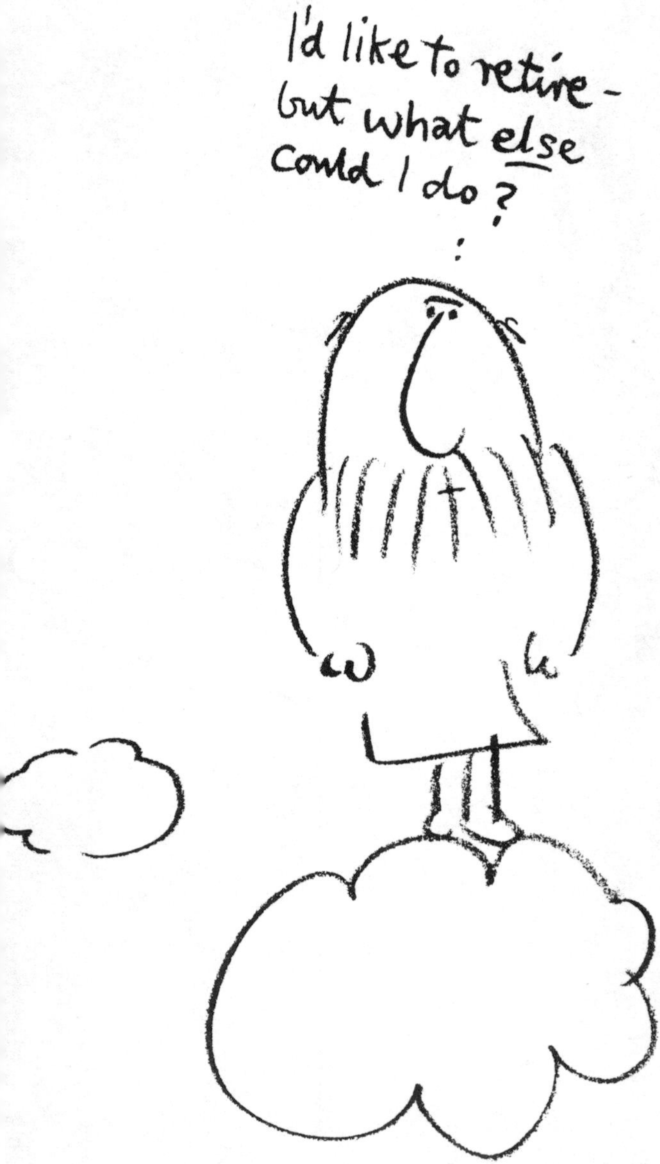
I'd like to retire - but what else could I do ?

it's a great strain being
omnipotent all
the time..

somedays everything
goes well and I'm glad
I'm God

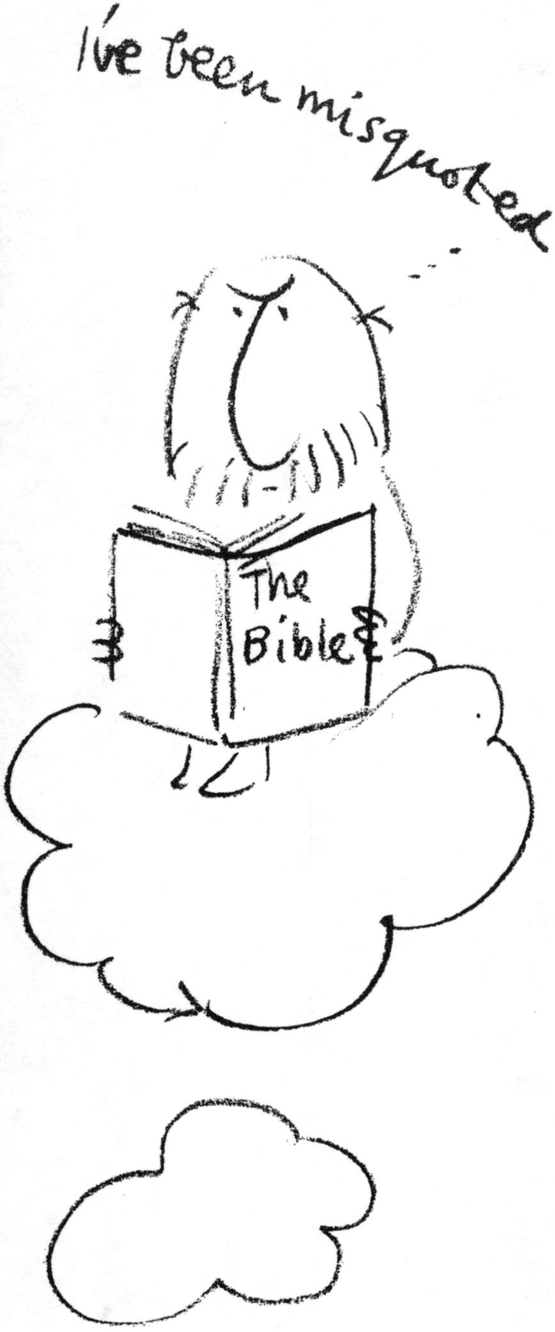
I've been misquoted . . .
The Bible

I should have known –
create in haste,
repent at leisure..

it's not fair -
everyone else has
a day off except
me.

Eternity is a long time to have to stay in one job.